Mug Cakes

Sweet & Savory Recipes

WHITE STAR PUBLISHERS

Photographs and Recipes
CINZIA TRENCHI

Project Editor
VALERIA MANFERTO DE FABIANIS

Graphic Design
MARIA CUCCHI

SWEETS...   12

Cookie mug cake	14
Mug cake with rice flakes, vanilla and chocolate	16
Lemon mug cake	18
Banana and vanilla mug cake	20
Mug cake with apple cream	22
Hazelnut cream and white chocolate mug cake	24
Mug cake with ricotta cream and mixed berries	26
Mug cake with strawberries and spelt flakes	28
Peanut and chocolate mug cake	30
Mug cake with chocolate, orange and lemon	32
Chocolate and whipped cream mug cake	34
Mug cake with egg cream and oat flakes	36
Mug cake with almond flour and honey	38
Prunes and dates mug cake	40
Mug cake with ricotta, honey and pistachio nuts	42

... AND VEGAN SWEETS   44

Cereal mug cake with hazelnut cream	46
Cereal mug cake with rice pudding and fruit	48
Rice flakes mug cake with blueberries and soy yogurt	50
Red fruit mug cake with millet	52
Cocoa mug cake with vanilla-flavored vegetable cream	54
Mug cake with chocolate, coconut, passito wine and banana	56
Dark chocolate mug cake with banana and chili	58
Millet mug cake with apple juice	60
Rice and oat milk mug cake	62
Mug cake with raisins and corn	64
Mug cake with pear, almonds and cinnamon	66
Mocha mug cake with vegetable whipped cream	68
Mug cake with rice pudding and apple	70
Mug cake with strawberries and cereals	72
Mug cake with mixed fruit, wine and maple syrup	74

The recipes

SAVORIES... 76

... AND VEGAN SAVORIES 108

Introduction

Let's face it: we have less and less free time – time left over from work, studying, and being with our family. Our free time is also often the time when we would like to cook. Cooking not only represents the preparation of meals, but it is also a pleasure, the idea of a well-being we believe in. That is why the chance to save a few minutes becomes very useful for preparing and trying out dishes to include in our diet.

We like our dishes to be light, low in sodium, with few fats, complete, or better still with appetizing and tasty organic ingredients. We must plan for 30 minutes to cook brown rice, 20 minutes for a risotto with plain rice, and at least half an hour for a pie. We crave for a flavor, and our mouths quickly begin to water. We'd like to have that delicious food in our teaspoon or on our fork immediately, ready to melt in the mouth giving us the taste that we are expecting!

Mug cakes become a delicious standby when we don't have a lot of time. Sweet and melting pies ready in 5 minutes for preparation and cooking, soups and pastas in 10 minutes, creams and pies that we only need to emulsify in a mug with a fork or a whisk... and voilà, long and complex preparations become extremely simple and fast! Of course, flavor purists can turn up their noses, but, when time is tight, any help is welcome.

This volume shows how easy it is to prepare so many little tempting morsels. They are able to satisfy our desire for sweet or savory, but not only. You will also find recipes for people who have cut animal proteins and their derivatives out of their diet. It's divided into four sections, so you can delve into rapid and appetizing recipes, from sweet to savory pies up to vegan ones. All in all, the guiding principle is how fast the recipes can be prepared. Then, we could not forget some "alternative" foods like millet, oats, brown rice, barley, and cereal flakes to go with seasonal fruit and vegetables, herbs and spices full of inviting aromas.

But what do we need to prepare a mug cake? First of all, a microwave oven, then exclusively Pyrex, porcelain, or ceramic mugs and cups, a whisk (you can buy any size, even very small), and a sieve for flour. With this elementary equipment, you can try out tempting recipes, so you can have a good alternative to a classic first course, a sandwich, or a dessert. Speaking of lack of time, microwave cooking is able to (at least) halve cooking times: for example, cooking plain rice takes about 8-10 minutes compared to the 20 we are used to. For a mug cake based on whole wheat flour with vegetables, 2-3 minutes is enough. What about a lentil mug cake cooked in 20 minutes, or a tempting dessert in 5 minutes including preparation time?

Some say that microwave cooking destroys the characteristics of food, while others say nutritional values are unaltered, because of the speed. What matters to us is a good, attractive, and tasty mug recipe with a good aroma: the mug cake is an excellent answer to our more frenetic lifestyles! The container chosen is not important. It must not have metallic elements, and can be any size you like, from an espresso coffee cup to the traditional cup for the cappuccino, to a mug... everything is possible to match the colors of the food to those of the container, for a tasty cake.

If you are just starting to bake mug cakes, you must reckon with a different baking process, which moves from the inside toward the outside and creates a certain "overflow". This means the cake rises, and if you don't cover the preparation with a film and the mug is more than two thirds full, the cake tends to come out of the container. In addition, this system of baking is recommended for small quantities of food, and the choice of mug is fundamental for excellent results: in fact, not all containers are suitable for use in the microwave oven. We must not use casseroles and pans – we should prefer mugs and glasses, except those with rims or decorations in silver, gold or metals in general. It is better for the container not to exceed a certain diameter (3-4 inches).

Finally, it is useful to remember that the baking time increases if several dishes are baked together. In preparations with vegetables, we advise you to precook them or cook them in liquids so that cooking does not dehydrate them. You can, indeed you should, use film to protect the natural humidity of the foods.

One clear advantage is that the cooking time is reduced. Another advantage – remember that you can mix ingredients with a fork or a small whisk in the container chosen for cooking and serving: this considerably reduces the number of cooking utensils, leaving the kitchen relatively tidy and with few things to wash up!

To try your skill at these recipes, at first it is useful to know that some foods react better to microwave cooking. Eggs, butter, sugar and flour are perfectly suitable and with a pinch of baking powder produce exciting cakes in just a few minutes. Vegetables and fruit mixed with flour work better than alone. You do not even need to grease the rim of the mug to have a cake that comes out without sticking! But straightaway there is the question: can we prepare the same recipes in the traditional oven?

Yes, certainly. The timing and the preparation change (the container must always be greased so the cake does not stick, and the cooking times are twice as long or more), but it can be a useful alternative until you own a microwave!

Don't forget

1. Always keep the microwave instruction booklet handy. It is useful to consult the suggestions at any moment. In fact, the operational principle is always the same, but the controls for power, accessories, times, dimension, and performance are different.

2. The microwave must never be switched on before use, and it must not be used empty: the microwaves could hit the walls inside and damage it.

3. If the microwave has the grill function, don't use plastic containers for cooking.

4. Use only materials compatible with the microwave: porcelain, ceramic, terracotta, Pyrex, suitable plastics, greaseproof paper, film. Avoid metals, old cups with hand decorations and materials containing lead.

5. When you purchase white, colored, or glass containers, check that they are guaranteed for microwave cooking.

6. When you cook rice, vegetables, seeds, legumes, etc. in water, always cover with a film suitable for the microwave but never hermetically seal it, as the container could explode, leaving food all over the oven! Always make a few small holes in the film with a toothpick.

7. It is preferable to cook one preparation at a time, since this kind of cooking is meant for small quantities.

8. To prepare the recipe perfectly, it is very important to follow cooking times, and also to consider the cooling times afterwards.

9. If you're not very familiar with the volume and weight of foods, obtain a small scale which lets you also weigh the ingredients in very small quantities, like powdered raising agents and spices.

10. Preparations in the mug lead to an immediate approach to foods. You can use a tablespoon or a teaspoon to measure the ingredients. For example, the correspondences to a level tablespoon are: 0.5 fluid ounces of liquids (10–12 ml); 0.28 ounces of cocoa (8 g); 0.3 ounces of flour (10 g); 0.5 ounces of sugar (12 g); 0.7 ounces of honey (20 g). Correspondences to the teaspoon: 0.17 ounces of salt (5 g), 0.14 ounces of baking powder (4 g). The ideal way to find out weight and quantity is to measure with its own spoon and make a personal table based on it.

Sweets...

The objective of this chapter is to prepare a dessert in 5 minutes, but to make it easily with a few utensils, so as to have something sweet without having to clear up afterwards! It doesn't matter much whether it is based on fruit, or other ingredients. The essential thing is to satisfy that sudden urge for something sweet that often assails us when we don't have time to get down to cooking. What makes the difference in these cases is the microwave's ease of use, also for complex recipes. It is so simple that trying out dishes, or rather "mugs", becomes child's play, with just a few precautions to avoid mistakes. It is possible to create variants starting from tried and tested recipes, using what is in the larder: there are in fact so many ingredients that lend themselves to microwave cooking!

Cookie mug cake

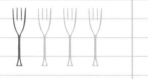

Servings

2-3 shortbread cookies (the number depends on the dimensions) – 2 tbsp of hazelnut cream (40 g) – 0.3 oz of milk chocolate (10 g) – 1/2 glass of milk (about 1.7 fl oz/0.5 dl)

Difficulty

Prep Time
5 minutes

Cooking Time
1 minute

1. Crumble the cookies and put them in a mug of your choice. Chop up the chocolate and mix it with the hazelnut cream and the cookies. Lastly, add the milk.

2. Cook in the microwave for 1 minute at 700 watts, then take out and leave to cool for 1 minute before enjoying it.

3. This is a standby sweet that you can prepare with what you find in the larder. You can replace hazelnut cream with chocolate cream, add chopped dried fruit or use a liqueur instead of the milk.

Mug cake with rice flakes, vanilla and chocolate

Servings

1 glass of milk (about 3.4 fl oz/1 dl) – 1 vanilla bean –
1 egg yolk – 1 tbsp of brown sugar (10 g) – 0.7 oz of
milk chocolate (20 g) – 4 tbsp of puffed rice (20 g)

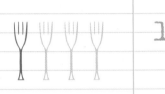

Difficulty

Prep Time
5 minutes

Cooking Time
40 seconds
+ 1 minute

1. Boil the milk with the chopped-up vanilla bean. You can do it directly in the microwave, for about 40 seconds at 700 watts. Then filter and leave to cool.

2. Beat the egg yolk with the sugar. Pour the milk, the beaten yolk and the puffed rice in a mug, cover with the broken-up chocolate and cook in the microwave for about 1 minute, wait 1 minute and serve.

3. An excellent nourishing and appetizing alternative, ideal for the first meal of the day for children and students.

Lemon mug cake

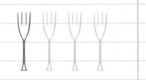

Servings

1 egg yolk – 1 organic lemon – 4 tbsp of lemon juice (about 0.4 dl) – 4 tbsp of soft wheat flour (about 40 g) – 1 tbsp + 1 tsp of melted butter (20 g) – 2 tbsp of sugar (about 20 g) – 1/2 tsp of baking powder for desserts (about 2 g)

Difficulty

1. Beat the egg yolk with the sugar, add the flour and, to make it easier to work with the mixture, pour in the lemon juice, the melted butter and finally the baking powder.

2. Wash the lemon and cut it into 3 or 4 thin slices, or even more: the quantity of sliced lemon depends on your liking for sour flavors.

3. Before you put the cake in the microwave, decorate it with the sliced lemon. Cook for 2 minutes at 700 watts, then check with a toothpick to see if it is done: if necessary, cook for 10 more seconds. Leave to cool for 1 minute before enjoying it.

Prep Time
5 minutes

4. This cake with a fresh, light flavor is dedicated to people who love sweets which are not too sweet!

Cooking Time
2 minutes

Banana and vanilla mug cake

Servings

1 banana – 1 glass of milk (about 3.4 fl oz/1 dl) – 1 tbsp + 1 tsp of butter (20 g) – 1 vanilla bean – 1 level tbsp of caster sugar (10 g) – 1 tbsp of coconut flour (8-10 g) – 3 tbsp of soft wheat flour (30 g) – 1/2 tsp of baking powder for desserts (2 g)

Difficulty

Prep Time
8-10 minutes

Cooking Time
2 minutes

1. Peel the banana and crush it with the prongs of a fork until you obtain a smooth purée.

2. Boil the milk with the chopped-up vanilla bean, then filter and add the butter; once it has perfectly melted, add the sugar, the banana, the flours and the baking powder.

3. Mix directly in the mug, cook in the microwave at about 600–700 watts for 2 minutes, and then check with a toothpick to see if the cake is of the desired consistency inside.

4. If it is not completely cooked, turn the microwave on for 10 or 15 more seconds, and then take out and leave to cool for a couple of minutes before you enjoy it.

Mug cake with apple cream

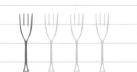

Servings

1 apple - 1 glass of apple juice (about 3.4 fl oz/1 dl) - 2 heaped tbsp of millet flour (about 30 g) - 2 tbsp of potato starch (about 10 g) - 1 tbsp of caster sugar (about 10-12 g) - 1 egg - 1/2 tsp of baking powder for desserts (about 2 g)

Difficulty

1. Wash the apple, slice half of it, leaving the skin, and blend the rest.

2. Beat the egg with the sugar and add the blended apple, and then all the other ingredients, except for the apple slices, which you will use for decoration.

Prep Time
6-8 minutes

3. Distribute the mixture between the two mugs not filling more than half or two thirds of the container.

4. Distribute the apple slices between the two mugs and cook them separately for about 2 minutes each at 700 watts.
If you want to cook the two portions together, put the containers well-separated in the microwave and bake for 4 minutes.

Cooking Time
2 minutes

Hazelnut cream and white chocolate mug cake

Servings

1 egg – 1 tbsp of unsweetened cocoa powder (about 10 g) – 2 tbsp of hazelnut flour (about 25 g) – 1 tbsp + 2 tsp of brown sugar (20 g) – 1 oz of white chocolate (30 g) – 2-3 tbsp of rum (if desired)

Difficulty

1. Grate the chocolate irregularly with a grater or a knife. Beat the sugar with the egg until you obtain a frothy mixture, by working on the ingredients directly in the mug with a fork or a small whisk.

2. Add the cocoa and the hazelnut flour little by little.

3. Lastly, if desired, add the rum, little by little.

Prep Time
5 minutes

4. Cook in the microwave for 2 minutes at 700 watts, then take out the mug, decorate with white chocolate and enjoy.

5. A magnificent dessert rich in flavor and aromas: it is perfect for a moment of intense pleasure.

Cooking Time
2 minutes

Mug cake with ricotta cream and mixed berries

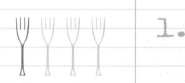

Servings

3.5 oz of raspberries and blueberries (100 g) – 3.5 oz of ricotta cheese (100 g) – 2 tbsp of potato starch (about 20 g) – 1 tbsp of caster sugar (about 12 g) – 1 egg – 3-4 tbsp of milk (about 0.4 dl)

Difficulty

1. Pour the ricotta into a bowl and beat it with the sugar and the egg until you obtain a soft and smooth mixture. Add the potato starch. If the cream is too thick, you can dilute it with a few tablespoons of milk, one at a time.

2. Wash the fruit, set some aside for decoration and add the rest to the cream.

3. Divide the mixture into two mugs of your choice and cook in the microwave for 2 minutes at 700 watts, then take them out, leave to cool for 1 minute, decorate with the fruit that you have set aside, and serve.

4. A dessert with a wonderful aroma, an ode to the cheerful colors of summer, this sweet not only satisfies our sense of taste but is also a treat for us to see and smell!

Prep Time
8 minutes

Cooking Time
2 minutes

Mug cake with strawberries and spelt flakes

Servings

1/2 cup of spelt flakes (50 g) – 3.5 oz of strawberries (100 g) – 2 tbsp of sugar (30 g) – 1/3 cup + 2 tbsp of whole milk yogurt (100 g)

Difficulty

1. Hull the strawberries, cut them into small pieces and cook them for 2 minutes in the microwave at maximum power, then take them out and leave to cool.

2. Mix the yogurt and the strawberries, the spelt and the sugar, divide the mixture between two mugs.

Prep Time
5 minutes

3. Cook each mug in the microwave again at 700 watts for 30 seconds, the time necessary for the heat to combine the various ingredients, then take the mugs out, leave to cool for 1 minute and serve.

4. Ideal for a tasty breakfast or a peppy snack.

Cooking Time
2 1/2 minutes

Peanut and chocolate mug cake

Servings

1 egg – 1 glass of milk (about 3.4 fl oz/1 dl) – 4 tbsp of soft wheat self-rising flour (45 g) – 2 level tbsp of brown sugar (20 g) – 1 tbsp of unsweetened cocoa powder (10 g) – 1 tbsp of peanut butter (20 g) – 20 peanuts

Difficulty

1. Shell the peanuts and also get rid of the inner skin. Beat the egg with the sugar and gradually add the other ingredients until you obtain a smooth mixture with no lumps.

2. Divide the mixture into two mugs, not filling more than half or two thirds of the container so that the cake doesn't overflow.

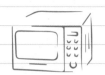

Prep Time
8-10 minutes

3. Decorate with the peanuts and cook the mugs one at a time at 700 watts for 2 minutes. Before you take them out of the microwave, check with a toothpick to see if they're done. If not, cook for 10 more seconds until you achieve the desired consistency.

4. Leave to cool for at least 1 minute before serving.

Cooking Time
2 minutes

Mug cake with chocolate, orange and lemon

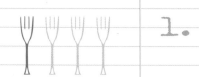

Servings

1 egg yolk – 1 glass of milk (about 3.4 fl oz/1 dl) – 2 level tbsp of brown sugar (20 g) – 1 tbsp of unsweetened cocoa powder (10 g) – 1 tbsp of soft wheat flour (10 g) – 1 tbsp + 1 tsp of melted butter (20 g) – 1 organic orange – 1 lemon

Difficulty

1. Wash the fruit, slice half of it finely and set it aside for decoration. Remove the zest from the rest and cut it into small pieces.

2. Beat the sugar with the egg yolk, add the flour and the cocoa and pour in the milk little by little. Finally, add the butter.

**Prep Time
6-8 minutes**

3. Once you have obtained a smooth mixture with no lumps, flavor it with part of the zest, mix again and divide it into two mugs. Cook them in the microwave, being careful to separate them enough.

4. You will need about 3 minutes at maximum power to cook both the mugs, or 1 and a half minutes at 700 watts per mug. Leave to cool for 1 minute, then decorate with the citrus slices and some pieces of zest and serve.

**Cooking Time
1 1/2 minute**

Chocolate and whipped cream mug cake

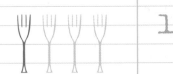

Servings

2 glasses of milk (about 6.6 fl oz/2 dl) – 1 1/2 tbsp of unsweetened cocoa powder (15 g) – 2 tbsp of sugar (25 g) – 1 tbsp of potato starch or soft wheat flour (10 g) – whipped cream (if desired)

Difficulty

Prep Time
8 minutes

Cooking Time
1 1/2 minute

1. Mix the cocoa powder, the sugar and the flour in a bowl. Add the milk little by little, stirring continuously, so that lumps do not form.

2. When you have obtained a smooth mixture, divide into two mugs and cook them in the microwave separately for 1 and a half minutes at 700 watts. Leave to cool for 1 minute, then distribute the whipped cream as you wish and serve.

3. It is an extremely pleasant, soft and creamy sweet, but you could make it still more tempting if you include two teaspoons of rum and a pinch of chili!

Mug cake with egg cream and oat flakes

Servings

1 egg yolk – 1 glass of milk (about 3.4 fl oz/1 dl) – 1 1/2 tbsp of oat flour (15 g) – 2 tbsp of oat flakes (10 g) – 1 tbsp of caster sugar (10 g) – 1/2 tsp of baking powder for desserts (2 g)

Difficulty

1. Beat the egg yolk with the sugar directly in a mug of your choice. Add the oat flour, the milk, half the flakes and the baking powder, and mix together.

2. When you have obtained a smooth mixture, sprinkle the remaining oat flakes onto the top and cook in the microwave for 2 minutes at 700 watts, then take out and leave to cool for 1 minute before serving.

3. This preparation is a splendid breakfast. If you leave a piece over, you can preserve it and enjoy it later at room temperature.

**Prep Time
5 minutes**

**Cooking Time
2 minutes**

Mug cake with almond flour and honey

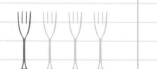

Servings

1 egg – 1 tbsp + 1 tsp of butter (20 g) – 3 tbsp of soft wheat self-rising flour (30 g) – 2 tbsp of almond flour (20 g) – 1 tbsp of honey (20 g) – 10 almonds

Difficulty

1. Put the butter in a mug and melt it in the microwave (a few seconds are enough), leave to cool slightly, add the egg and mix with half the honey.

2. Add the self-rising flour and the almond flour (set a little aside for decoration).

Prep Time
5 minutes

3. Mix with a fork or a small whisk, until you obtain a smooth mixture with no lumps. Cover with the almonds, the honey and the almond flour that you have set aside.

4. Cook in the microwave at 700 watts for 2 minutes and leave to cool for a couple of minutes. When the cakes are taken out of the microwave, the cooking continues due to the effect of the accumulated heat.

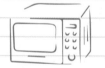

Cooking Time
2 minutes

Prunes and dates mug cake

Servings

1 glass of orange juice (about 3.4 fl oz/1 dl) – 2 level tbsp of soft wheat flour (about 20 g) – 2 tbsp of mixed cereals (about 25 g) – 2 stoneless dates – 2 stoneless prunes – 1 tbsp + 1 tsp of melted butter (20 g) – 1 orange slice – 1/2 tsp of baking powder for desserts (about 2 g)

Difficulty

1. Mix the flour with the orange juice and add the butter.

2. Cut the prunes and the dates into little pieces. Add to the flour the fruit, the cereals and the baking powder. When all the ingredients are well mixed, pour into the mug and put it in the microwave.

3. Cook for 2 minutes at 700 watts, then take out. Decorate with a slice of orange, leave to cool for 1 minute before enjoying it.

**Prep Time
8 minutes**

4. A marvelous sweet, perfect also for a nourishing and satisfying breakfast.

**Cooking Time
2 minutes**

Mug cake with ricotta, honey and pistachio nuts

Servings

3.5 oz of ricotta cheese (100 g) - 1 heaped tbsp of soft wheat flour (about 15 g) - 1 oz of shelled pistachios (30 g) - 1 tbsp + 1 tsp of butter (20 g) - 1 tbsp of Millefiori honey (about 20 g) - 1/2 tsp of baking powder for desserts (about 2 g)

Difficulty

Prep Time
5 minutes

Cooking Time
2 minutes

1. Roughly chop the pistachios.

2. In the microwave, melt the butter in the mug that you will use to prepare the dessert (10 seconds at 400 watts is enough), then take out of the oven; add and mix with a fork the flour, the honey, the baking powder, half the ricotta and half the pistachios.

3. Separately, work with a whisk the remaining ricotta and put in the rest of the pistachios.

4. Cook the mug cake in the microwave for 2 minutes at 700 watts, then leave to cool for 1 minute.

5. Cover the mug cake with the ricotta and pistachios mixture and enjoy.

... and Vegan Sweets

The trend to reduce the consumption of foods of animal origin or to decide to become vegan is getting more and more common, both for ethical reasons and for your physical well-being. In this book we could not forget recipes dedicated to this lifestyle. Certainly, it seems strange to think of cutting eggs, butter, sugar, and milk out of sweets. Yet, for example, by replacing and supplementing these ingredients with malt, maple syrup, soy butter, and drinks based on cereals like oats and rice, we obtain excellent, decidedly healthy, sweets. Also in this case, the microwave can help. Its speed helps us to make savory pies, hashes and flans in record time, while we can rely on carefully chosen ingredients. The recipes suggested in this section are ideal for breakfast, a snack or a relaxing break. They are perfect recipes for adults and children.

Cereal mug cake with hazelnut cream

3 tbsp of puffed wheat (about 35 g) – 10 hazelnuts –
2 tbsp of hazelnut cream (40 g) – 3 tbsp of soy milk
(0.3 dl)

1. Shell the hazelnuts and chop them roughly.
Put all the ingredients in a Pyrex mug and
mix them with a fork.

2. Cook in the microwave at 700 watts for about
1 minute, the time necessary to blend the
ingredients, then leave to cool for 30 seconds
and serve.

3. In this tempting dessert, we make up for the lack
of sugar by the richness of the soft fats and
the nutritional principles of the hazelnuts and
the cream.

Cereal mug cake with rice pudding and fruit

Servings

1 heaped cup of mixed cereals in flakes (about 30 g) – 1.7 oz of rice pudding (50 g) – 1.7 oz of blueberries (50 g) – 4 raspberries and 4 strawberries – 2 plums – 1/2 pear – 2 tbsp of maple syrup (10 g)

Difficulty

Prep Time
8 minutes

Cooking Time
2 minutes

1. Wash all the fruit, hull the strawberries, peel the pear. Cut the pear and the plums into small pieces, then set them aside.

2. Mix the cereals with the rice pudding, the blueberries, the strawberries, the raspberries and the maple syrup. Stir and divide the mixture into two mugs not filling more than half full.

3. Cook in the microwave for 2 minutes at 700 watts; then take out, leave to cool for 1 minute, cover with the mixed pear and plums and serve.

4. A magnificent breakfast or a substitute for a quick lunch, extremely light, alternates the warmth and softness of the cereal mixture with the fresh fruit.

Rice flakes mug cake with blueberries and soy yogurt

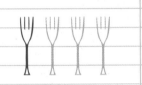

Servings

1 scant cup of rice flakes (about 20 g) – 3.5 oz of blueberries (100 g) – 3 tbsp + 1 tsp of soy yogurt (50 g) – 1/2 glass of apple juice (about 1.7 fl oz/0.5 dl)

Difficulty

Prep Time
10 minutes

Cooking Time
1 minute

1. Wash the blueberries and drain them in a colander. In a bowl, mix the rice flakes, the yogurt and the apple juice together with the fruit.

2. Divide the mixture between two mugs and cook in the microwave for 1 minute at 700 watts. The more you keep the mixture in the microwave, the more the flakes will soften and blend with the other ingredients: be careful not to cook them too much – they will become spongy and dry!

3. A magnificent snack rich in flavor and decorated with blueberries, whose color is enhanced by the very rapid cooking.

Red fruit mug cake with millet

Servings

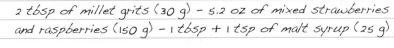

2 tbsp of millet grits (30 g) – 5.2 oz of mixed strawberries and raspberries (150 g) – 1 tbsp + 1 tsp of malt syrup (25 g)

Difficulty

Prep Time
15 minutes

Cooking Time
10 minutes

1. Wash the strawberries and the raspberries delicately without submerging them in the water, hull the strawberries and leave them to dry on a paper towel.

2. In the meantime, cook the millet in the microwave, putting the grits in a container with double their volume of water. You will need about 8 minutes at maximum power. Then leave to cool.

3. Combine the millet and the malt syrup, pour the mixture into a mug of your choice which is suitable for microwave cooking, not filling more than half full, and insert some pieces of strawberry and raspberry.

4. Cook in the microwave for 2 minutes at 700 watts, and serve with the remaining fruit.

5. It smells and tastes good and is tempting with the fresh flavor of spring. It is the perfect sweet for any moment of the day.

Cocoa mug cake with vanilla-flavored vegetable cream

Servings

1 1/2 tbsp of unsweetened cocoa powder (15 g) – 2 tbsp of soft wheat self-rising flour (20 g) – 1/2 cup + 5 tbsp of soy vegetable cream (200 g) – 1 tbsp + 1 tsp of melted soy butter (20 g) – 1 glass of rice milk (about 3.4 fl oz/1 dl) – 1 tbsp + 1 tsp of malt syrup (25 g) – 2 vanilla beans

Difficulty

1. Crush a vanilla bean in the rice milk and boil it (you need about 1 minute in the microwave at maximum power), then leave to cool. Crush the other bean and mix it with the soy cream.

2. Add the cocoa to the flour, then pour in little by little the flavored milk, the butter, the malt syrup and cook in the microwave. The time depends on the size of the mug, and on whether you prefer the cake hard or soft.

3. We advise you to start cooking only for a few minutes and to cook again after checking: 2 minutes at 600 watts per mug should be enough. Serve with the vegetable cream.

Prep Time
5 minutes

Cooking Time
3 minutes

Mug cake with chocolate, coconut, passito wine and banana

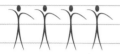

Servings

1 small banana - 2 tbsp of slivered almonds (about 10 g) - 1.8 oz of dark chocolate (50 g) - 1 tbsp of coconut flour (10 g) - 1 small glass of passito wine or another dessert wine (about 1.7 fl oz / 0.5 dl)

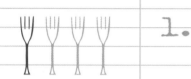

Difficulty

Prep Time
5 minutes

Cooking Time
2 minutes

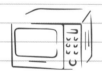

1. Break up the chocolate, put it in a mug and melt it in the microwave (about 1 minute at maximum power).

2. Peel the banana, cut it into pieces, add it to the passito wine and the coconut flour and mix gently.

3. When the chocolate is warm, work it with a fork, add the mixture with the banana and cook for 1 minute at 600 watts. Take out of the oven and sprinkle the slivered almonds onto the top.

4. A magnificent dessert to conclude a lunch or an important dinner. Simple but tasty, it is prepared in just a few minutes.

Dark chocolate mug cake with banana and chili

Servings

2 baby bananas - 2 tbsp of soft wheat flour (20 g) - 2 tbsp of unsweetened cocoa powder (20 g) - 2 glasses of soy milk (about 6.6 fl oz/2 dl) - 1 tbsp + 2 tsp of malt syrup (30 g) - 1 dried chili per person

Difficulty

1. Peel the bananas and cut them into rounds. Wash the chilies and dry them. Dissolve the cocoa and the malt in the mixture of flour and milk. Use a whisk to mix the ingredients.

2. When the mixture is smooth and with no lumps, add the banana and all or part of the chili, according to your liking for hot things.

3. Divide the mixture into four small mugs and cook in the microwave for 50 seconds at 700 watts, then take them out, leave them to cool for 30 seconds and serve.

4. Super simple and quick to prepare, or rather super quick, it is a perfect mixture of flavors which is able to satisfy the most demanding palates, in spite of the very few calories!

Prep Time
6-7 minutes

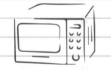

Cooking Time
50 seconds

Millet mug cake with apple juice

1/4 cup of millet flour (30 g) – 1/4 cup of cornstarch (30 g) – 1 glass of apple juice (about 3.4 fl oz/1 dl) – 2 tbsp of corn oil (20 g) – 1 apple – 2 tbsp of pine nuts (about 20 g) – 1 tbsp of maple syrup (15 g)

Difficulty

1. In a bowl, mix the flours, then add the apple juice and the oil; when you have an even mixture, divide it between two mugs not filling more than half full.

2. Wash the apple, cut it into little pieces with the skin and put them in the mugs. Remember that the apple will stay crunchy in comparison with the other ingredients, but the contrast with the softness of the rest will be pleasant.

3. Garnish the top with maple syrup and pine nuts, and cook each mug in the microwave for 2 minutes at maximum power. Leave to cool for 1 minute and serve.

Prep Time
10 minutes

Cooking Time
2 minutes

Rice and oat milk mug cake

Servings

3.5 oz of rice (100 g) – 1 tbsp of dried red fruits (about 15 g) – 1 glass of oat milk (about 3.4 fl oz/1 dl) – 1 glass of almond milk (about 3.4 fl oz/1 dl) – 1 tbsp of slivered almonds (about 10 g) – 1 1/2 tbsp of almond flour (10 g)

Difficulty

1. Wash the rice several times and cook it in the microwave in 6.7 fluid ounces of water for 8 minutes at 700 watts, then take it out and leave to cool for 2 minutes.

2. Add the oat milk, the almond milk, the red fruits and the almond flour and mix until the ingredients are completely blended.

**Prep Time
8-10 minutes**

3. Divide the mixture into two mugs and cook separately for 2 minutes or together for 4 minutes, in both cases at 700 watts.

4. Take them out of the microwave, leave to cool for 1 minute, garnish with the slivered almonds and serve.

**Cooking Time
10 minutes**

5. A delicious, naturally sweet mixture, it is the perfect alternative for a meal.

Mug cake with raisins and corn

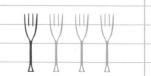

Servings

1/4 cup of cornstarch (30 g) – 2 heaped tbsp of soft wheat self-rising flour (30 g) – 2 tbsp + 2 tsp of soy butter (40 g) – 1 glass of rice milk (about 3.4 fl oz/1 dl) – 1 tbsp + 1 tsp of malt syrup (20 g) – 1 tbsp of pine nuts (about 10 g) – 2 tbsp of raisins (about 15 g)

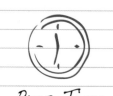

Difficulty

Prep Time
5-6 minutes

Cooking Time
2 minutes

1. Soak the raisins in half a glass of warm water. Then drain them, but keep the water to dilute the flours.

2. Melt the soy butter and add it to the cornstarch, mix, dilute with the rice milk and add the self-rising flour. If the mixture is too hard or difficult to work with, pour in the water from the raisins little by little.

3. Finally, add half the raisins, half the pine nuts and all the malt syrup. Mix again and divide into two mugs. Complete the sweet by sprinkling the pine nuts and the raisins that you have set aside.

4. Cook for 2 minutes at 700 watts per mug, then check with a toothpick to see if it is cooked, leave to cool for 1 minute and serve.

Mug cake with pear, almonds and cinnamon

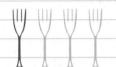

Servings

1/4 cup of oat flour (20 g) – 1 tbsp of soft wheat flour (10 g) – 1 tbsp of maple syrup (15 g) – 1/2 glass of pear juice (about 1.7 fl oz/0.5 dl) – 1/2 pear – 1 tbsp of corn oil (10 g) – 1/2 tsp of baking powder for desserts (2 g) – 1/2 tsp of cinnamon powder (2 g) – 1 tsp of slivered almonds (about 5 g)

Difficulty

1. Wash the pear and cut it into small pieces.

2. Mix the flours with half the cinnamon, pour in little by little the pear juice, the oil, half the maple syrup and finally add the baking powder. Mix until it is smooth and with no lumps.

3. Half fill the mug and garnish with the little pieces of pear. Pour in the remaining maple syrup, complete with the remaining cinnamon and the almonds.

**Prep Time
5-6 minutes**

4. Cook in the microwave for 2 minutes at 700 watts, then check with a toothpick to see if it is cooked. If it does not seem to be totally done, cook for 10 more seconds.

5. This dessert smells great. It alternates different consistencies: the crunchiness of the pear and the softness of the rest of the mixture.

**Cooking Time
2 minutes**

Mocha mug cake with vegetable whipped cream

Servings

4 friable cookies – 1 tbsp of potato starch (10 g) – 1/2 glass of whiskey (about 1.7 fl oz/0.5 dl) – 3.5 fl oz of espresso coffee (about 1 dl) – 2 tbsp of malt syrup (30 g) – vegetable whipped cream (as much as you like) – 2 coffee beans to decorate

Difficulty

1. Crumble the cookies and distribute them into two mugs, sprinkling them with the liqueur.

2. Mix the coffee with about 3.5 fluid ounces of water (1 dl), the potato flour, and the malt syrup; pour the mixture onto the cookies, not filling the mugs more than half full.

Prep Time
5 minutes

3. Put in the microwave for 2 minutes at 700 watts, then take out, leave to cool for 1 minute, cover with the cream, decorate with the coffee bean and serve.

4. This dessert is perfect for a rich, intense pleasurable break or after dinner. The different consistencies and flavors complement one another, alternating tempting color tones.

Cooking Time
2 minutes

Mug cake with rice pudding and apple

Servings

3 tbsp + 1 tsp of soy cream (50 g) – 1 tbsp + 1 tsp of rice flour (15 g) – 1 apple – 2 tsp of maple syrup (10 g)

Difficulty

Prep Time
13 minutes

Cooking Time
12 minutes

1. Wash the apple, put it in a large mug and cook it in the microwave for about 10 minutes at 700 watts, or until it is soft.

2. Put into a mug the soy cream, the rice flour and the maple syrup, mix directly in the container with a small whisk and plunge the apple into the mixture.

3. Cook again in the microwave for 2 more minutes at maximum power, then leave to cool for 1 minute and serve.

4. A delicious sweet which smells captivating. The consistency of the apple may vary from crunchy to very soft; it is better if first you cook it separately, as all foods containing a lot of water need longer times than proteins and fats.

Mug cake with strawberries and cereals

Servings

4-6 strawberries – 1 scant cup of mixed cereal flakes (about 20 g) – 1 tbsp of oat cream (15 g) – 1/2 glass of apple juice (about 1.7 fl oz/0.5 dl)

Difficulty

1. Wash and hull the strawberries and cut them into pieces. Put the flakes, the apple juice and the strawberry pieces into a mug, mix, cover with the cream and put in the microwave.

2. Cook for 1 and a half minutes at 700 watts: in this time, the sweet will become compact and the fruit will blend with the cereals.

3. This light, fresh dessert is perfect for a nourishing breakfast. It smells very good, and it is naturally sweet thanks to the apple juice.

Prep Time
5 minutes

Cooking Time
1 1/2 minute

Mug cake with mixed fruit, wine and maple syrup

Servings

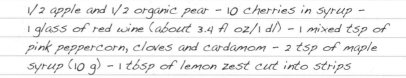

1/2 apple and 1/2 organic pear – 10 cherries in syrup – 1 glass of red wine (about 3.4 fl oz/1 dl) – 1 mixed tsp of pink peppercorn, cloves and cardamom – 2 tsp of maple syrup (10 g) – 1 tbsp of lemon zest cut into strips

Difficulty

Prep Time
8 minutes

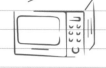

Cooking Time
2 minutes

1. Wash the apple and the pear and cut them into small pieces. If you like, you can leave the skin.

2. Put the fruit into a mug, add the wine, the cherries, the spices and the maple syrup, mix and cook in the microwave for 2 minutes at maximum power. The fruit will stay quite crunchy, so if you wish it to be softer, cook it for 1 or 2 more minutes.

3. Leave to cool for 1 minute, then garnish with the lemon zest and enjoy.

4. This dessert smells wonderful – it is rich and decidedly original, thanks to the spicy aroma of the pepper, cloves and cardamom, the sweetness of the syrup and the alcohol of the wine!

Savories...

Pizza flavor, Mediterranean scents, herbs, spices and chili. These are some of the tasty ingredients that are included in the recipes proposed in the section "Savories", fifteen very quick and easy mug cakes, with intriguing associations of flavors, to enjoy flans and savory pies in the mug. In this section of the book we suggest savories ready in record time, dishes that include important flavors, good, tasty recipes that thanks to an alternative cooking produce even surprising results in not much time. We can range from a tempting oregano flan ready in 8 minutes, to a melting cream of cheese and egg in 5, to a spinach savory pie in quarter of an hour! These times are surprising, if we consider that with traditional cooking we should double, if not triple, the cooking times! And the flavor? The microwave often enhances and emphasizes the aroma and flavor of foods due to the rapid cooking!

Spinach mug cake

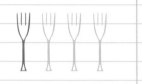

Servings

2 eggs – 2 glasses of light cream (about 6.7 fl oz/2 dl) – 1 oz of ricotta cheese (30 g) – 3 tbsp of soft wheat flour (30 g) – 1.7 oz of spinach leaves (50 g) – 1 tbsp of extra virgin olive oil (10 g) – salt and pepper

Difficulty

1. Wash the spinach, chop up about ten leaves and set them aside. Stew the rest in oil. You can cook it in the microwave at 600 watts for 2 minutes, adding a tablespoon of water so that the leaves do not dry, then leave to cool for 1 minute, drain the cooking water, if any, and chop up.

2. Beat the eggs with the cream, the ricotta, the flour, the stewed spinach, salt and pepper to taste. Pour into two mugs not filling more than half full.

Prep Time
15 minutes

3. Cook separately in the microwave for 2 minutes at 600 watts per mug, and check with a toothpick to see if it's evenly cooked. If you want the top to brown, choose the grill mode and cook the cakes for about 10 minutes, but first check the indications in your microwave's instruction booklet and remember not to use any plastic containers.

Cooking Time
4 minutes

4. Before you serve, garnish with the chopped spinach leaves that you have set aside.

Artichoke mug cake

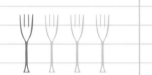

Servings

1 artichoke – 1 oz of ricotta cheese (30 g) – 1 tbsp of soft wheat flour (10 g) – 2 tbsp of milk (0.3 dl) – 1/4 cup of grated Parmigiano Reggiano (30 g) – 1 tbsp of extra virgin olive oil (10 g) – salt and pepper

Difficulty

Prep Time
15 minutes

Cooking Time
2 minutes

1. Wash the artichoke, take off the tough, hard outer leaves, cut the top third and steam it for 10 minutes. Then drain it and oil all the surface.

2. Mix the ricotta with half the Parmigiano Reggiano directly in a mug of your choice, add the milk and the flour, salt and pepper to taste and dip the artichoke in this cream.

3. Cook in the microwave for 2 minutes at 600 watts, take it out, dust with the remaining Parmigiano Reggiano, leave to rest for 1 minute and serve.

Legume mug cake

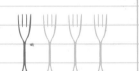

Servings

3/4 cup of soft wheat flour (80 g) – 1 tbsp of turmeric – 1 glass of water (about 3.4 fl oz/1 dl) – 10 pods of peas and 5 of fava beans – 2 tbsp of extra virgin olive oil (20 g) – 1 tsp of poppy seeds (3 g) – 1 tsp of baking powder for savories (4 g) – salt and pepper

Difficulty

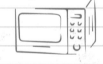

Prep Time
10 minutes

Cooking Time
3 minutes

1. Shell the legumes, rinse and drain them in a colander. Dissolve the turmeric in 3 tablespoons of water.

2. Mix in a large mug (suitable for two people) the flour and the baking powder and pour in the necessary water in spoonfuls to obtain a soft, smooth mixture with no lumps. Season with the oil, salt and pepper to taste.

3. Add the legumes, sprinkle the poppy seeds onto the top and cook in the microwave at 700 watts for 3 minutes. Leave to cool for 1 minute, then take the cake out of the oven and slice it.

4. This cake is very particular: the legumes stay crunchy and the dough is soft. So it is perfect to replace bread or to go with salads and vegetables in general.

Tomato and caper mug cake

Servings

1 egg – 3 *tbsp of soft wheat flour* (30 g) – 1 1/2 *tbsp of extra virgin olive oil* (15 g) – 10 *salted capers* – 1/2 *tsp of baking powder for savories* (2 g) – 2 *ripe firm plum tomatoes* – *salt and pepper*

Difficulty

1. Wash the tomatoes and cut them into small pieces. Drain off any excess water in a colander. Soak the capers in water to remove the salt, then rinse repeatedly under running water. Dab them with a paper towel and chop half of them finely.

2. Mix the flour with the baking powder and the egg. Dilute with 2 tablespoons of water and, if necessary, add more, but always only one tablespoon at a time. The mixture must be smooth, sticky and with no lumps. Lastly, add the other half of the capers not chopped, a tablespoon of oil, salt and pepper to taste.

**Prep Time
10 minutes**

3. In a mug of your choice, make a base with half the tomato pieces, half the chopped capers and half a tablespoon of oil.

4. Pour the mixture in it and cover with the remaining tomato and the whole capers. Cook in the microwave for 2 minutes at 700 watts.

**Cooking Time
2 minutes**

5. A magnificent contrast of consistencies and scents, all Mediterranean!

Leek mug cake

Servings

2 eggs – 1 leek – 1 glass of milk (about 3.4 fl oz/1 dl) – 1 heaped tbsp of soft wheat flour (about 15 g) – 1/4 cup of grated Parmigiano Reggiano (30 g) – 1 pat of butter (about 0.7 oz/20 g) – salt and pepper

Difficulty

Prep Time
12 minutes

Cooking Time
8 minutes

1. Prepare the leek by washing it and throwing away any hard leaves and the hard top; then cut it into rings.

2. Melt the butter with the leek (set a few rings aside for decoration) and gently stew them together. You can use the microwave, adding two tablespoons of water and initially cooking for 4 minutes at 600 watts. Then check the consistency to make sure it is how you want it. Remember that vegetables taken from the microwave must rest for 2 minutes, in which the cooking will continue.

3. Drain off any cooking water from the leek. Beat the eggs with the Parmigiano Reggiano, add the flour, the milk, then the stewed leek, salt and pepper and mix.

4. Pour the mixture into a mug, cover with the leek rings and cook in the microwave for 4 minutes at 600 watts. Then leave to rest for 2 minutes, take it out of the mug, divide into portions and serve.

Mug cake with ham and cheese

Servings

2/3 cup of soft wheat flour (60 g) – 1 glass of milk (about 3.4 fl oz/1 dl) – 1 egg – 2 tbsp of corn oil (20 g) – 1.4 oz of Fontina cheese (40 g) – 1 egg – 2 slices of ham (about 1.4 oz/40 g) – 1/2 tsp of baking powder for savories (2 g) – salt and pepper

Difficulty

1. Divide the Fontina in half, grate one half and cut the other into small pieces.

2. Mix the flour with the milk, the egg, the oil and half the Fontina, both in small pieces and grated. When you have obtained a soft, smooth mixture with no lumps, add salt and pepper to taste.

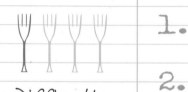

**Prep Time
10 minutes**

3. Add the baking powder and line the inside of the two mugs with slices of ham. Pour in the mixture not filling more than half or two thirds full.

4. If the ham goes over the rim of the mugs, don't worry: it will be absorbed by the cake in cooking.

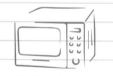

**Cooking Time
2 minutes**

5. Cook in the microwave for 2 minutes per mug at 700 watts, then leave it to rest for 1 minute, sprinkle with the remaining Fontina and serve. This extremely appetizing cake is excellent if you enjoy it as soon as it is prepared, but also at room temperature. It can replace a first course or constitute a nourishing breakfast.

Mug cake with stracchino cream and egg

Servings

1 egg – 1.7 oz of stracchino cheese or another creamy cheese (50 g) – 2 tbsp of light cream (0.25 dl) – salt and pepper

Difficulty

1. In the bottom of a mug put a tablespoon of cream, place half the stracchino on it and break the egg directly onto the cheese.

2. Add the remaining cheese and cream. Season with a pinch of salt and plenty of pepper.

3. Cook in the microwave for 2 minutes at 400 watts, then leave to cool for 1 minute and serve.

4. This cake stays soft and melting: it is a triumph of flavors which enhance each other. Very quick and simple to prepare and perfect as a treat appetizer.

Prep Time
5 minutes

Cooking Time
2 minutes

Mediterranean mug cake

Servings

1 egg – 1/2 glass of milk (about 1.7 fl oz/0.5 dl) – 3 tbsp of soft wheat flour (30 g) – 1 small tomato – 1/2 red onion – 1 sprig of fresh oregano – 1 tbsp of extra virgin olive oil (10 g) – salt

Difficulty

Prep Time
8 minutes

Cooking Time
3 minutes

1. Prepare the vegetables, chop the onion finely and slice the tomato.

2. Put the egg, the milk, the flour, the oil, and the salt in a mug; stir until you obtain a smooth mixture with no lumps.

3. Add the onion and some oregano leaves and stuff the cake with the tomato slices.

4. Cook in the microwave for 3 minutes at 600 watts, then check with a toothpick to see if it's done. If necessary, cook for 10 or 15 more seconds, until you achieve the desired consistency. Leave to rest for 2 minutes and enjoy it.

5. This cheerful mug cake with its appetizing colors immerses you in the scents of summer.

Pumpkin and pink peppercorn mug cake

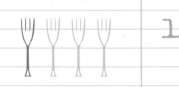

Servings

1/4 cup of barley (50 g) - 2 cabbage leaves - 3.5 oz of pumpkin (100 g) - 1.4 oz of ricotta cheese (40 g) - 1/2 tsp of pink peppercorn - 1 tbsp of extra virgin olive oil (10 g) - salt

Difficulty

Prep Time
15 minutes

Cooking Time
12 minutes

1. Wash the cabbage leaves and cut them into small strips. Remove the zest and any strands from the pumpkin and cut it into small pieces. Mix the vegetables with the ricotta.

2. Rinse the barley several times under running water, then cook it in the microwave at maximum power for 10 minutes in double its volume of water. Leave to rest for 2 minutes and drain it, then season with the oil.

3. Add the vegetables to the barley, salt to taste, scent and flavor with the pink peppercorns, pour into a mug and cook in the microwave for 2 minutes at 700 watts.

4. An excellent fragrant and tasty first course. It alternates the softness of the cereal and the crunchiness of the vegetables.

Zucchini and cheese mug cake with borage

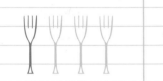

Servings

3 tbsp of soft wheat flour (30 g) – 1/2 glass of milk (about 1.7 fl oz/0.5 dl) – 1.7 oz of stretched curd cheese (50 g) – 5 borage leaves – 1 small zucchini – 1 egg – 1/2 tsp of baking powder for savories (2 g) – salt and pepper

Difficulty

Prep Time
6-7 minutes

Cooking Time
2 minutes

1. Wash the zucchini, cut off the ends and chop it up. Wash the borage leaves and chop them up finely. Cut the cheese into pieces.

2. Mix the flour and the egg; pour in little by little the milk and the baking powder directly in the mug of your choice working them with a whisk or a fork. Add the chopped zucchini and the borage.

3. Add salt and pepper to taste, plunge the cheese in the mixture and cook in the microwave for 2 minutes at maximum power, then leave to rest for 1 minute. Decorate with edible flowers or herbs and serve.

4. This recipe, which perfectly combines the consistency of the vegetables and the softness of the dough, is an excellent idea to replace a complete meal. If you wish, you can take the cake out of the mug and serve it in slices, accompanying it with a salad.

Eggplant Parmesan mug cake

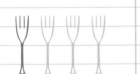

Servings

8 thin slices of grilled eggplant – 3.5 oz of braided mozzarella (100 g) – 2 small ripe tomatoes – 2 sprigs of fresh mint – 2 tbsp of extra virgin olive oil (20 g) – salt and pepper

Difficulty

Prep Time
5 minutes

Cooking Time
2 minutes

1. Wash the mint, take the leaves of one sprig and chop them, then put them in a dish with oil, salt and pepper to taste, and mix.

2. Wash the tomatoes and slice them. Then dip the tomato and eggplant slices in the aromatized oil. Slice the mozzarella.

3. Take a mug of your choice and alternate the various flavors: eggplant, tomato, mozzarella (set a piece aside) and cook in the microwave for 2 minutes at 700 watts, then take out, garnish with the remaining mozzarella and mint, and serve.

4. An extremely fresh, light recipe, in which the consistencies combine and the intense scent of mint goes perfectly with the other ingredients.

Mug cake with cornstarch, sausage and tomato

Servings

2 tbsp of soft wheat flour (20 g) – 3 tbsp of cornstarch (30 g) – 6 cherry tomatoes – 2.8 oz of sausage (80 g) – 1 tbsp of extra virgin olive oil (10 g) – 1/2 tsp of baking powder for savories (2 g) – salt and pepper

Difficulty

**Prep Time
6-7 minutes**

**Cooking Time
2 minutes**

1. Wash the tomatoes and cut them into small pieces. Take the casing off the sausage.

2. Mix the flours, then put in the baking powder, add the oil and 3 or 4 tablespoons of water little by little, to obtain a soft, smooth mixture.

3. Combine the sausage with the tomatoes, mix, add salt and pepper to taste, but remember that the sausage is already seasoned!

4. Divide the mixture into two mugs and cook separately in the microwave for 2 minutes at 700 watts per mug. Then take out, leave to rest for 1 minute and serve.

5. This mug cake is perfect for preparing a lunch or dinner in record time!

Mug cake with shrimps and zucchini

Servings

2 zucchini – 2 dried tomatoes – 4 fresh shrimp tails –
2 heaped tbsp of sour cream (0.3 dl) – 2 sprigs of parsley
– 2 tbsp of extra virgin olive oil (20 g) – salt and pepper

Difficulty

Prep Time
10 minutes

Cooking Time
2 minutes

1. Wash and dry the parsley. Pour the oil into a dish and add salt and pepper to taste.

2. Wash the zucchini and slice them lengthwise with a potato peeler. Then dip them in the seasoned oil. Soak the dried tomatoes in warm water, then drain. Eliminate the carapace from the shrimps and wash them. Leave to dry on a paper towel and dip them in the oil.

3. Arrange the appetizer in two high coffee cups, wrapping the zucchini slices around the tomato and shrimps. Cook in the microwave for 2 minutes at 600 watts, then leave to cool for 30 seconds. Flavor with the sour cream and the sprigs of parsley and serve.

4. It is a fragrant little appetizer, which alternates soft and crunchy consistencies, perfect for an attractive and elegant aperitif.

Mug cake with bacon, cheese and asparagus

Servings

4 tbsp of soft wheat flour (40 g) - 4 slices of bacon - 2 boiled potatoes - 1.7 oz of ricotta cheese (50 g) - 1/4 cup of grated Parmigiano Reggiano (30 g) - 4 asparagus - 1 egg - 2 tbsp of corn oil (20 g) - 1/2 tsp of baking powder for savories (2 g) - 4 tsp of milk (0.2 dl) - salt and pepper

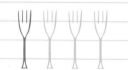

Difficulty

1. Wash the asparagus and cut them into rounds, discarding the hard, woody part.

2. Mash the potatoes until they are soft and smooth. Put in the egg, the ricotta, the flour, the oil, the Parmigiano Reggiano and the baking powder. Stir the ingredients to obtain a soft, even mixture. If it's too thick, dilute with the milk.

Prep Time
10 minutes

3. Season with salt and pepper to taste. Add two thirds of the asparagus to the mixture. Cover the inside of the mugs with the bacon slices and pour the mixture in, not filling more than half full. Garnish with the remaining asparagus. In cooking, the bacon exposed will be absorbed by the cake.

Cooking Time
2 minutes

4. Cook each mug in the microwave for 2 minutes at 700 watts, then leave to rest for 1 minute before serving.

Spicy shrimp mug cake with habanero

Servings

1 egg – 1/2 cup of soft wheat flour (60 g) – 6 shrimp tails – 1 tbsp of extra virgin olive oil (10 g) – 1 small habanero chili – 1 tsp of baking powder for savories (4 g) – salt

Difficulty

Prep Time
10 minutes

Cooking Time
2 minutes

1. After removing the carapace from the shrimp tails, cut them into small pieces.
Wash the chili and use it according to your liking for hot flavors.

2. Mix the flour with the baking powder, the egg, the oil, and the salt, and stir, pouring in one tablespoon of water at a time until you obtain a soft, smooth mixture with no lumps. Add the chili and the shrimps and mix again.

3. Divide into two mugs and cook separately in the microwave at 700 watts for 2 minutes per mug. If the mixture is too liquid and the mug is full, the cake will tend to overflow, but if you take it out of the microwave it will become firmer and drop slightly. Leave to rest for 1 minute before serving.

4. The habanero is one of the hottest existing chilies, but also among the most aromatic. This mug cake is tempting and appetizing, perfect to nibble together with vegetables and salads or to accompany fish main courses.

... and Vegan Savories

Whole wheat flour, millet, rye and oats are some of the ingredients for preparing savory pies and flans. They are for people who try to complete their diet with foods promoting greater well-being. This is associated with seasonal vegetables, as an alternative to animal proteins, to respect our planet. Of course, also here we have looked for tasty ideas to solve the problem of our lifestyle: no time! Time-saving mug cakes which follow the vegan diet - they come out fragrant and appetizing in 5 or 15 minutes at the most for preparation and cooking. Lastly, let's not forget that the advantage of preparing mug cakes is that you can achieve little dishes for one or two people. This means you can reduce left-overs and waste.

Cauliflower mug cake with millet flour and oat cream

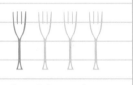

Servings

1.7 oz of oat flour (50 g) – 1.7 oz of millet flour (50 g) – 3.5 oz of cauliflower and broccoli florets (100 g) – 7 tbsp of oat cream (1 dl) – 1 heaped tbsp of sesame seeds (10 g) – 1 tbsp of extra virgin olive oil (10 g) – 1 tsp of baking powder for savories (4 g) – Hawaiian salt

Difficulty

1. Prepare the broccoli and the cauliflower, then chop them.

2. Mix the flours and put in the baking powder, then pour in the oat cream little by little and blend until you obtain a soft mixture.

3. Add the oil together with the vegetables and pour the mixture into two mugs. Sprinkle the top with the Hawaiian salt and the sesame seeds.

Prep Time
8 minutes

4. Cook in the microwave for 2 minutes at 700 watts, then take out, leave to rest for 1 minute and serve.

5. When the mugs are almost full, the mixture will tend to come out. If you also wish to shape the overflowing part, you can insert parchment paper as protection between the inside of the mug and the mixture.

Cooking Time
2 minutes

Thyme, zucchini and sunflower seeds mug cake

3.5 oz of boiled and drained millet (100 g) – 3 scant tbsp of soy cream (0.4 dl) – 2 tomatoes – 1 small zucchini – 4 sprigs of thyme – 1 tbsp of sunflower seeds (8 g) – 4 tbsp of extra virgin olive oil (40 g) – salt and pepper

1. Wash the zucchini, cut off the ends and cut it into small pieces.

2. Wash the tomatoes and cut them according to your imagination. Prepare the thyme, cut off the hard parts and cut it up finely.

3. Mix the millet, the cream, 2 tablespoons of oil, half the vegetables, and salt and pepper to taste.

4. Divide the mixture into two mugs, sprinkle half a tablespoon of sunflower seeds on the top and cook in the microwave for 2 minutes at 600 watts. Then leave to rest for 1 minute, garnish with the vegetables, the remaining sunflower seeds and oil, the thyme and serve.

5. This recipe can constitute an excellent first course and is characterized by the contrast between the creaminess of the millet and the crispness of the vegetables.

Herb mug cake

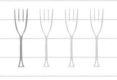

Servings

3 tbsp of whole wheat flour (30 g) – 1 tbsp of soft wheat flour (15 g) – 1 small spring onion – 1 bunch of mixed herbs (parsley, sage, oregano, marjoram) – 1/2 glass of rice milk (about 1.7 fl oz/0.5 dl) – 2 tbsp of extra virgin olive oil (20 g) – 1/2 tsp of baking powder for savories (2 g) – salt and pepper

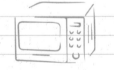

Difficulty

1. Prepare the herbs and the spring onion, wash, dry and chop them.

2. Mix the flours and put in the baking powder (you can use the mug chosen for the cake directly). Pour in the rice milk little by little and, when you have a soft, smooth mixture with no lumps, add the chopped herbs.

3. Season with salt and pepper to taste, complete the mug cake with a tablespoon of oil mixed with the other ingredients, and pour the other tablespoons of oil on the top.

4. Cook in the microwave for 2 minutes at maximum power, then check with a toothpick (which must come out clean) to see if it's evenly cooked, and serve. If you leave it to cool and turn it out, it can be sliced and served as a complement to a salad or a vegetable dish.

Prep Time
7 minutes

Cooking Time
2 minutes

Mug cake with onion, nettle and barley

Servings

1/4 cup of pearl barley (50 g) – 3.5 oz of nettle tips (100 g) – 1 onion – 4 tbsp of soy cream (0.5 dl) – 2 tbsp of extra virgin olive oil (20 g) – salt and pepper

Difficulty

Prep Time
15 minutes

Cooking Time
13 minutes

1. Prepare the nettles, take off the hard parts and keep only the leaves. Boil them in water for 2 minutes in the microwave at maximum power, drain and leave to cool.

2. Peel the onion and slice it finely, then mix it with the nettles, the oil and the cream.

3. Wash the barley several times in water (this predisposes it for cooking), then boil it in twice its volume of salted water in the microwave for 10 minutes at maximum power. Leave to rest for 3 minutes, check the consistency and drain off any excess water.

4. Blend the mixture with the seasoning, add salt and pepper to taste and place it the microwave again for 1 minute at 600 watts. Leave to rest for 1 minute and serve.

5. Normally it would take longer to cook a dish like this, but thanks to the microwave it is possible to enjoy it also when there is little time.

Mug cake with oat flakes, sunflower seeds and fava beans

Servings

4 tbsp of oat flakes (about 20 g) – 3 tbsp + 1 tsp of rye flour (20 g) – 4 tbsp of soy Béchamel (0.5 dl) – 4 pods of fava beans – 1 tsp of sunflower seeds (about 3 g) – 1 tsp of coriander seeds (about 1 g) – 1 tbsp of extra virgin olive oil (10 g) – 1/2 tsp of baking powder for savories (2 g) – salt and pepper

Difficulty

1. Shell the fava beans, mix the oat flakes with the flour, the baking powder and the oil, and add the Béchamel one tablespoon at a time. If necessary, add a tablespoon of water too, to obtain a soft mixture.

2. Put in the fava beans, half the coriander and the sunflower seeds, salt and pepper to taste; cover the mixture with the remaining seeds.

**Prep Time
5 minutes**

3. Cook in the microwave for 2 minutes at maximum power, then take it out, leave to rest for 1 minute and serve.

4. Fragrant and full of taste, it is a mug cake that can replace a snack or a first course, and also bread, if you leave it to cool and cut it into slices.

**Cooking Time
2 minutes**

Mug cake with zucchini blossoms and oat cream

Servings

7 tbsp of oat flour (40 g) – 1 small zucchini – 4 zucchini blossoms – 3 tbsp + 1 tsp of oat cream (50 g) – 2 tbsp of extra virgin olive oil (20 g) – 1 tsp of baking powder for savories (4 g) – salt and pepper

Difficulty

Prep Time
10 minutes

Cooking Time
2 minutes

1. Prepare the zucchini blossoms and cut them into little pieces. Wash the zucchini and chop it finely.

2. Mix the flour with the oil, the cream and, if the mixture should be too thick, dilute with 2 tablespoons of water.

3. Put in the baking powder and, when you have a smooth mixture with no lumps, add the zucchini, the blossoms, and salt and pepper to taste.

4. Divide the mixture into two mugs and cook them separately for 2 minutes at 700 watts or together for 4 minutes. Then take out and leave to rest for 1 minute before serving.

5. In microwave cooking, the resting time is very important. The cooking continues in this time: so, don't be deceived if the cake looks too soft when it is taken out, but wait patiently for the resting time to end, and you will see that the cake will be completely done!

Cabbage mug cake

6 cabbage leaves – 1 purple spring onion – 1 dried chili – 6 tbsp of rye flour (40 g) – 2 tbsp of extra virgin olive oil (20 g) – 1/2 tsp of baking powder for savories (2 g) – soy sauce – salt

Difficulty

Prep Time
8-10 minutes

Cooking Time
3 minutes

1. Wash the cabbage leaves and chop finely two of them. Prepare the spring onion, cut it into rounds (including the green part) and combine two thirds with the cabbage.

2. Put the baking powder into the rye flour, and mix in about 1 fluid ounce of water, adding it little by little. Salt to taste, add the cut and chopped vegetables, the oil, the chili and mix again.

3. Line a sufficiently large mug with the remaining cabbage leaves, pour in the mixture and cover with the cabbage, as if it were a paper cone.

4. Cook in the microwave for 3 minutes at 700 watts, then leave to rest for 1 minute and serve accompanied by soy sauce flavored with the remaining spring onion.

5. It is a very tasty mug cake, with the cabbage that maintains its freshness and color. The filling is a fine union of crisp vegetables and the soft rye.

Mug cake with corn kernels, rice and oat Béchamel

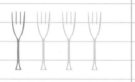

Servings

1.7 oz of Basmati rice (50 g) - 1 oz of boiled corn (30 g) - 3.5 oz of cauliflower florets (100 g) - 1 tbsp + 1 tsp of soy butter (20 g) - 2 tbsp of oat cream (30 g) - salt and pepper

Difficulty

1. Prepare the cauliflower and cut it into pieces a little larger than corn kernels. Combine them with the corn (set some pieces aside for decoration), then add salt and pepper to taste and pour in the oat cream.

Prep Time
12 minutes

2. Wash the rice several times under running water, and boil it in the microwave in twice its volume of salted water for 8 minutes at 700 watts; then leave to rest for a couple of minutes.

3. Drain off any excess water, blend with the vegetables, add the butter and cook in the microwave for 1 minute at 600 watts. Then leave to cool, complete with the pieces of cauliflower that you have set aside and serve.

Cooking Time
9 minutes

4. This mug cake alternates the softness of the rice with the crispness of the cauliflower in a magnificent contrast of consistencies, colors, and flavors.

Whole wheat flour mug cake with dried tomatoes, oregano and capers

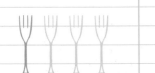

Servings

4 tbsp of whole wheat flour (40 g) – 10 salted capers – 2 dried tomatoes – 1 tsp of gomashio – 1/2 chili in powder – 1 sprig of oregano – 2 tbsp of extra virgin olive oil (20 g) – 1/2 tsp of baking powder for savories (2 g)

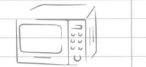

Difficulty

Prep Time
10 minutes

Cooking Time
2 minutes

1. Soak the dried tomatoes in warm water; after 5 minutes, drain them and blend together with the oil.

2. Soak the capers in water to remove the salt, then rinse repeatedly under running water. Drain and dry them, then chop finely.
Wash the oregano and, after dabbing it dry, chop it and combine with the capers together with the chili and half the gomashio.

3. Stir the flour with 3 or 4 tablespoons of water until you obtain a smooth, soft and sticky mixture. Add the baking powder, the tomato blend and the chopped capers; mix to amalgamate the flavors.

4. Pour the mixture into a mug, not filling it more than two-thirds full and cook in the microwave for 2 minutes at 700 watts, then leave to rest, decorate with herbs and edible flowers and serve.

5. This mug cake is perfect to replace bread, with much shorter preparation time! If you leave it to cool, you can take it out and slice it to accompany vegetable dishes and sauces.

Mixed flour mug cake with broccoli, sesame and chili

Servings

4 tbsp of whole wheat flour (40 g) – 2 tbsp + 2 tsp of millet flour (20 g) – 2 tbsp of cornstarch (20 g) – 3.5 oz of broccoli (100 g) – 1 tbsp of sesame seeds (8 g) – 1 dried chili – 2 tbsp of extra virgin olive oil (20 g) – 1 tsp of baking powder for savories (4 g) – salt

Difficulty

1. Prepare the broccoli and cut it into small pieces. Crumble the chili.

2. Put in the flours, add the baking powder, then pour in about half a glass of water, one tablespoon at a time. If you wish, you can prepare the cake directly in the mug.

3. When the mixture is soft and smooth, add the broccoli, the oil, half tablespoon of sesame, and half the chili to taste and blend together. Lastly, sprinkle the top with the remaining sesame and chili and salt to taste.

Prep Time
8-10 minutes

4. Cook in the microwave for 3 minutes at 700 watts, then take out, leave to rest for 2 minutes and serve. An excellent substitute for a first course or for bread, if you leave it to cool and cut it into slices.

Cooking Time
3 minutes

Lentil and carrot mug cake

3.5 oz of softened lentils (100 g) – 1 carrot – 2 cloves of garlic – 1 leek – 1 sprig of rosemary – 2 tbsp of oat cream (30 g) – 2 tbsp of extra virgin olive oil (20 g) – salt and pepper

Difficulty

Prep Time
20-22 minutes

Cooking Time
17 minutes

1. Chop the rosemary finely. Prepare the carrot and the leek, and cut them into small pieces.

2. Wash the lentils several times under running water; boil them in the microwave, with half the vegetables and the garlic cloves, at maximum power for 15 minutes in twice their volume of salted water.

3. Then take out of the microwave, drain off any excess cooking water, discard the garlic, add salt and pepper to taste.
Put in the remaining vegetables, the oat cream, the oil, mix and cook in the microwave again for 2 minutes at 700 watts. Take out, leave to rest for 2 minutes and serve.

4. The fragrance of this mug cake is magnificent: besides stimulating the appetite, it can be prepared in record time compared to traditional cooking. If you wish to use canned lentils, the time is even shorter!

Millet and Swiss chard mug cake with chili

Servings

6 tbsp of millet (60 g) – 1.7 oz of Swiss chards (50 g) – 1 carrot – 1 zucchini – 1 small tomato – 2 tbsp of extra virgin olive oil (20 g) – 1 dried chili – salt and pepper – 1 lemon (optional)

Difficulty

Prep Time
15 minutes

Cooking Time
11 1/2 minutes

1. Wash all the vegetables and cut them into small pieces. Parboil the chard tops in salted water and drain them when they are soft.

2. Wash the millet and boil it for 10 minutes in the microwave in twice its volume of salted water; take it out and immediately blend it with the vegetables, also adding the chard tops.

3. Season with the oil, the salt, the pepper, and the chili; cook in the microwave again for 1 and a half minutes at 700 watts, then leave to rest for 2 minutes before serving.

4. An excellent mixture of colors, consistencies and flavors, perfect to replace a first course if eaten hot, or a salad if eaten cold, seasoned with the juice from a freshly squeezed lemon.

Whole wheat pasta mug cake with dried fruit and soy Béchamel

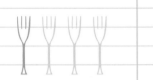

Servings

2.4 oz of whole wheat pasta (70 g) – 1 tbsp of mixed pine nuts and almonds – 1 tbsp of raisins (about 7 g) – 4 tbsp of soy Béchamel (0.5 dl) – salt and pepper

Difficulty

Prep Time
5-6 minutes

Cooking Time
3 minutes

1. Soak the raisins in warm water, then drain them. Cook the pasta in the microwave in twice its volume of salted water for 2 minutes at 700 watts.

2. Then take it out, leave to rest for a moment, and drain. Mix it with the soy Béchamel, the dried fruit, and the raisins; add salt and pepper, put it in a mug and cook it in the microwave for 1 minute at 600 watts. Then leave to cool for 1 minute and serve.

3. An excellent first course, very quick to prepare, it perfectly combines the neutral flavor of the pasta with the sweetness of the raisins and the spiciness of the pepper.

Rice mug cake with spices and walnuts

Servings

3.5 oz of rice (100 g) – 1 onion – 8 walnut kernels –
4 sprigs of thyme – 1 1/2 tbsp of curry (10 g) – 4 tbsp of
soy cream (0.5 dl) – 2 tbsp of extra virgin olive oil (20 g) –
salt

Difficulty

1. Peel the onion and slice it finely. Dissolve the curry in the soy cream and mix.

2. Wash the rice several times under running water and cook it in the microwave at maximum power for 8 minutes in twice its volume of salted water. Leave to rest for 1 minute and drain off any excess water.

Prep Time
10-12 minutes

3. Mix the rice with the leaves from 2 thyme sprigs, the curry cream, the oil, salt to taste and the walnuts, and divide into two mugs.
   Cook each mug for 1 minute at maximum power, then leave to rest for 1 minute, decorate with the remaining thyme leaves and serve.

4. This is a fragrant and appetizing first course abounding with intermingling colors and flavors. It's a risotto that is prepared in very short time.

Cooking Time
9 minutes

Rice mug cake with bell peppers and peas

Servings

1.7 oz of Basmati rice (50 g) – 1 oz of shelled peas (30 g) – 1 spring onion – 1/4 of red bell pepper – 3 scant tbsp of soy Béchamel (0.3 dl) – 1 tbsp of extra virgin olive oil (10 g) – salt and pepper

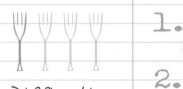

Difficulty

Prep Time
10 minutes

Cooking Time
10 minutes

1. Prepare the spring onion and the pepper, wash and dry them and cut into small pieces.

2. Cook the rice in the microwave in twice its volume of salted water for 8 minutes at maximum power, then leave to rest for 2 minutes, drain and mix with the Béchamel and the oil.

3. Add the vegetables and the peas, then salt and pepper to taste, mix again, and put in a mug without worrying about filling it too much: the mixture will maintain its volume during cooking without overflowing.

4. Cook in the microwave for 2 minutes at 600 watts, then leave to rest for 1 minute before serving.

5. What people like in this dish is the magnificent contrast between the softness of the rice and the crispness of the vegetables, which stay almost raw and maintain their fresh flavor.

The author

CINZIA TRENCHI, is a naturopath, journalist, and freelance photographer. She specialized in nutrition and enogastronomic trails, and collaborates on many cookbooks from publishers in Italy and abroad. A passionate cook, she has worked for many years with various Italian magazines, revisiting regional, traditional, macrobiotic and natural cooking specialties, supplying content and photographs and suggesting dishes she has conceived. Her cookbooks propose original and creative diets, associating flavors and trying out unusual combinations that give rise to new dishes inspired by taste. She always remembers the nutritional characteristics of the foods to achieve a greater balance at table and a consequent improvement in well-being. She lives in in Montferrat, in Piedmont, in a house deep in the country. She prepares sauces and original condiments with flowers, herbs, and the produce from her vegetable garden, which she also uses to decorate her dishes. She is guided by the seasons and her knowledge of the fruits of the earth. White Star Publishers has published these books by her in English:" Gluten- Free Gourmet Recipes"; "Fat-Free Gourmet Recipes"; "Chili Pepper: Moments of Spicy Passion"; "My Favorite Recipes", "Smoothies & Juices: Health and Energy in a Glass", "Superfoods: Healthy, Nourishing and Energizing Recipes" and "Detox: Practical Tips and Recipes for Clean Eating."

Index of Ingredients

WHITE STAR PUBLISHERS

WS White Star Publishers® is a registered trademark
property of De Agostini Libri S.p.A.

© 2016 De Agostini Libri S.p.A.
Via G. da Verrazano, 15
28100 Novara, Italy
www.whitestar.it - www.deagostini.it

Translation: Jonathan West, Kathryn Lake
Editing: ICEIGEO, Milano (Margherita Giacosa, Paola Paudice, Federica Guarnieri)

ISBN 978-88-544-1019-0
1 2 3 4 5 6   20 19 18 17 16

Printed in China